S Diabetic Snacks

D0194478

Snacks can be good for you!

Eating healthy is important for everyone. It is especially important for people with diabetes because it can have a great impact on your blood sugars. By carefully choosing what and when you eat, you can help maintain healthy blood sugar levels and reduce your risk of complications from diabetes. Your blood sugars can fluctuate up and down throughout the day and eating well-portioned snacks can help you control them. Snacking is often referred to as "bad for you"; however, it can be an important part of a daily meal plan for a person with diabetes.

Follow these tips when choosing your snacks.

- Choose whole grain snacks. Whole grains are rich in fiber and complex carbohydrates, which give you energy.

- Choose fruits and vegetables. Eating fruits and vegetables provides a feeling of fullness with no fat and only a small amount of calories. They also provide vitamins, minerals and fiber.

- Choose nuts and seeds. They provide protein, fat and vitamin E. Be careful with the quantity because they can be high in calories.

- Choose low-fat or non-fat dairy. Cheese, yogurt and other dairy products are good sources of calcium and protein.

Nutritional Analyses

Each recipe comes with the nutritional information you need to determine how the food will affect your blood sugar, as well as how it will fit with your calorie, fat and sodium goals. The nutritional values for the recipes in this book were calculated by an independent nutrition consulting firm. The Dietary Exchanges are based on the Exchange Lists for Meal Planning, developed by the American Diabetes Association, Inc. and the American Dietetic Association.

Every effort has been made to check the accuracy of these numbers. However, because numerous variables account for a wide range of values in certain foods, all analyses that appear in this book should be considered approximate. Unless otherwise specified, the nutritional calculations were also based on the following:

- Each analysis is based on a single serving of the recipe.

- Optional ingredients and garnishes were not included.

- If a range is given for an ingredient, the lesser amount was used. If an ingredient is presented with an option (e.g., 2 cups hot cooked rice or noodles), the first item listed is the one used.

- In photographs, extra foods shown on the same serving plate with the food of interest were not included.

- Meats were trimmed of all visible fat. Cooked rice, pasta and noodles were prepared without added salt and fat.

- Moderation, portion sizes and meal planning are the keys to success with any healthful eating plan.

dipped & spread

Garlic Bean Dip

  4 cloves garlic
  1 can (about 15 ounces) pinto or black beans, rinsed
    and drained
  ¼ cup pimiento-stuffed green olives
  4½ teaspoons lemon juice
  ½ teaspoon ground cumin
    Assorted fresh vegetables and crackers (optional)

1. Place garlic in food processor; process until minced. Add beans, olives, lemon juice and cumin; process until well blended but not entirely smooth.

2. Serve with vegetables and crackers, if desired.

Makes 12 servings (about 1½ cups)

Note: Cumin is a widely used spice in Middle Eastern, Asian and Mediterranean cooking. It is available in both seed and ground forms and adds a nutty flavor to dishes.

Hint: Prepared fresh vegetables, such as carrots, celery and bell peppers are typically housed in the produce section of supermarkets.

Prep Time: 10 minutes

Nutrients per Serving (2 tablespoons dip [without vegetables and crackers]):
Calories: 42, **Calories from Fat:** 21%, **Total Fat:** 1g,
Saturated Fat: <1g, **Cholesterol:** 0mg, **Sodium:** 207mg,
Carbohydrate: 7g, **Dietary Fiber:** 1g, **Protein:** 3g

Dietary Exchanges: ½ Starch

Nutty Carrot Spread

¼ cup finely chopped pecans
6 ounces cream cheese, softened
2 tablespoons frozen orange juice concentrate, thawed
¼ teaspoon ground cinnamon
1 cup shredded carrots
¼ cup raisins
36 toasted slices party pumpernickel bread or melba toast rounds

1. Preheat oven to 350°F. Place pecans in shallow baking pan. Bake 6 to 8 minutes or until lightly toasted, stirring occasionally. Cool slightly.

2. Meanwhile, combine cream cheese, juice concentrate and cinnamon in small bowl; stir until well blended. Stir in carrots, pecans and raisins.

3. Serve spread with toasted bread or melba toast.

Makes 18 servings

Nutrients per Serving (2 bread slices with about 2 tablespoons cream cheese mixture [about 1 tablespoon per slice]):
Calories: 68, **Calories from Fat:** 19%, **Total Fat:** 1g,
Saturated Fat: <1g, **Cholesterol:** 2mg, **Sodium:** 149mg,
Carbohydrate: 11g, **Dietary Fiber:** <1g, **Protein:** 3g

Dietary Exchanges: ½ Starch, ½ Fat

Asian Peanut Butter Dip

- 3 tablespoons reduced-fat creamy peanut butter
- 2 tablespoons apple butter
- 2 tablespoons fat-free (skim) milk
- 1 tablespoon reduced-sodium soy sauce
- 1½ teaspoons lime juice
- 10 stalks celery, cut into fourths

Combine peanut butter, apple butter, milk, soy sauce and lime juice in small bowl; whisk together until very smooth. Store, tightly sealed, in refrigerator. Serve with celery.

Makes 5 servings

Travel Tip: Divide dip between 5 individual resealable containers and cover tightly. Divide celery between 5 small resealable food storage bags. Store in a cooler packed with ice.

Nutrients per Serving (2 tablespoons dip with 8 celery pieces): **Calories:** 70, **Calories from Fat:** 21%, **Total Fat:** 3g, **Saturated Fat:** <1g, **Cholesterol:** <1mg, **Sodium:** 218mg, **Carbohydrate:** 10g, **Dietary Fiber:** 2g, **Protein:** 3g

Dietary Exchanges: ½ Fruit, 1 Vegetable, ½ Fat

tip

Apple butter is a richly flavored preserve made by slowly cooking apples, apple cider, sugar and spices together over low heat. It can be found with jams, jellies and honeys in most large supermarkets.

Chunky Hawaiian Spread

1 can (8 ounces) DOLE® Crushed Pineapple, well drained
½ cup fat free or light sour cream
1 package (3 ounces) light cream cheese, softened
¼ cup mango chutney*
Low fat crackers

If there are large pieces of fruit in chutney, cut them into small pieces.

• Beat crushed pineapple, sour cream, cream cheese and chutney in bowl until blended. Cover and chill 1 hour or overnight. Serve with crackers. Refrigerate any leftover spread in airtight container for up to one week.

Makes 2½ cups spread (20 servings)

Nutrients per Serving (2 tablespoons spread [without crackers]):
Calories: 28, **Calories from Fat:** 22%, **Total Fat:** 1g,
Saturated Fat: <1g, **Cholesterol:** 2mg, **Sodium:** 33mg,
Carbohydrate: 5g, **Dietary Fiber:** <1g, **Protein:** 1g

Dietary Exchanges: ½ Fruit

tip

Mango chutney is a tasty condiment popular in Indian cooking. A blend of mango, vinegar, sugar and spices, it adds a unique flavor to any dish. Chutneys are often located in the ethnic foods section of the supermarket.

Fast Guacamole and "Chips"

2 ripe avocados
½ cup chunky salsa
¼ teaspoon hot pepper sauce (optional)
½ seedless cucumber, sliced into ⅛-inch-thick rounds

1. Cut avocados in half; remove and discard pits (see tip below). Scoop flesh into medium bowl; mash with fork.

2. Add salsa and hot pepper sauce, if desired; mix well.

3. Transfer guacamole to serving bowl. Serve with cucumber "chips." *Makes 8 servings*

Nutrients per Serving (about 3½ tablespoons guacamole with cucumber "chips"):
Calories: 85, **Calories from Fat:** 72%, **Total Fat:** 7g,
Saturated Fat: 1g, **Cholesterol:** 0mg, **Sodium:** 120mg,
Carbohydrate: 5g, **Dietary Fiber:** 2g, **Protein:** 2g

Dietary Exchanges: 1 Vegetable, 1½ Fat

tip

To prepare an avocado, insert a knife into the stem end. Slice in half lengthwise, turning the avocado while slicing. Remove the knife blade and twist the avocado halves to pull apart. Insert the center of your knife blade into the pit with one sharp hacking motion. Twist slightly; the pit should come out easily.

Fresh Fruit with Creamy Lime Dipping Sauce

> 1 small jicama, peeled and cut into ½-inch-thick
>   strips, each about 3 to 4 inches in length
> 2 tablespoons lime juice
> 2 pounds watermelon, rind removed, cut into
>   ½-inch-thick wedges, each about 2 to 3 inches
>   wide
> ½ small pineapple, rind removed, halved lengthwise
>   then cut crosswise into wedges
> 1 ripe papaya, peeled, seeded and sliced crosswise
> Creamy Lime Dipping Sauce (recipe follows)

Toss jicama and lime juice in large bowl; drain. Arrange jicama, watermelon, pineapple and papaya on large platter. Serve with Creamy Lime Dipping Sauce.

Makes 12 servings

Creamy Lime Dipping Sauce

> 1 container (6 ounces) vanilla fat-free yogurt
> 2 tablespoons minced fresh cilantro
> 2 tablespoons lime juice
> 1 tablespoon minced jalapeño pepper*

*Jalapeño peppers can sting and irritate the skin, so wear rubber gloves when handling peppers and do not touch your eyes.

Combine all ingredients in small bowl; mix well.

Makes about 1 cup

Nutrients per Serving (¹⁄₁₂ of total recipe):
Calories: 65, **Calories from Fat:** 5%, **Total Fat:** <1g,
Saturated Fat: 0g, **Cholesterol:** <1mg, **Sodium:** 23mg,
Carbohydrate: 15g, **Dietary Fiber:** 1g, **Protein:** 1g

Dietary Exchanges: 1 Fruit

Berry Good Dip

8 ounces fresh strawberries or thawed frozen unsweetened strawberries
4 ounces fat-free cream cheese, softened
¼ cup reduced-fat sour cream
1 tablespoon sugar
Orange peel (optional)
Fresh fruit such as apple slices, strawberries, pineapple wedges and orange segments

1. Place strawberries in food processor or blender; process until smooth.

2. Beat cream cheese in small bowl until smooth. Stir in sour cream, strawberry purée and sugar; cover. Refrigerate until ready to serve.

3. Spoon dip into small serving bowl. Garnish with orange peel. Serve with assorted fresh fruit for dipping.

Makes 6 servings

Nutrients per Serving (¼ cup dip [without fruit dippers]):
Calories: 47, **Calories from Fat:** 16%, **Total Fat:** 1g,
Saturated Fat: <1g, **Cholesterol:** 7mg, **Sodium:** 120mg,
Carbohydrate: 6g, **Dietary Fiber:** 1g, **Protein:** 3g

Dietary Exchanges: ½ Fruit, ½ Lean Meat

Chutney Cheese Spread

2 packages (8 ounces each) fat-free cream cheese, softened
1 cup (4 ounces) shredded reduced-fat Cheddar cheese
½ cup mango chutney
¼ cup sliced green onions
3 tablespoons dark raisins, chopped
2 cloves garlic, minced
1 to 1½ teaspoons curry powder
¾ teaspoon ground coriander
½ to ¾ teaspoon ground ginger
1 tablespoon chopped dry-roasted peanuts
Toasted bread slices (optional)

1. Place cream cheese and Cheddar cheese in food processor or blender; process until smooth. Stir in chutney, green onions, raisins, garlic, curry powder, coriander and ginger. Cover; refrigerate 2 to 3 hours.

2. Sprinkle peanuts over spread just before serving. Serve with toasted bread, if desired.   *Makes 20 servings*

Variation: Try substituting 1 tablespoon toasted coconut for the peanuts in this recipe to give it a slightly sweeter flavor.

Nutrients per Serving (2 tablespoons spread topped with peanuts [without toasted bread slices]):
Calories: 58, **Calories from Fat:** 18%, **Total Fat:** 1g,
Saturated Fat: <1g, **Cholesterol:** 7mg, **Sodium:** 218mg,
Carbohydrate: 7g, **Dietary Fiber:** <1g, **Protein:** 5g

Dietary Exchanges: ½ Starch, ½ Lean Meat

Chutney Cheese Spread

Fresh Tomato Eggplant Spread

  1 medium eggplant
  2 large ripe tomatoes, peeled, seeded and chopped
  1 cup finely chopped zucchini
  ¼ cup chopped green onions
  2 tablespoons red wine vinegar
  1 clove garlic, minced
  1 tablespoon finely chopped fresh basil
  1 tablespoon olive oil
  2 teaspoons finely chopped fresh oregano
  1 teaspoon finely chopped fresh thyme
  1 teaspoon honey
  ⅛ teaspoon black pepper
  ¼ cup pine nuts or slivered almonds
  32 melba toast rounds

1. Preheat oven to 375°F. Poke holes in surface of eggplant with fork. Place in shallow baking pan. Bake 20 to 25 minutes or until tender. Cool completely. Peel and discard skin; finely chop eggplant. Place in colander; press to squeeze out excess liquid.

2. Combine eggplant, tomatoes, zucchini, green onions, vinegar, garlic, basil, oil, oregano, thyme, honey and pepper in large bowl; mix well. Cover; refrigerate 2 hours to allow flavors to blend.

3. Stir in pine nuts just before serving. Serve with melba toast rounds.   *Makes 8 servings*

Nutrients per Serving (⅛ of spread with 4 melba toast rounds):
Calories: 117, **Calories from Fat:** 31%, **Total Fat:** 4g,
Saturated Fat: 0g, **Cholesterol:** 0mg, **Sodium:** 65mg,
Carbohydrate: 15g, **Dietary Fiber:** 2g, **Protein:** 4g

Dietary Exchanges: ½ Starch, 1½ Vegetable, ½ Fat

Fresh Tomato Eggplant Spread

Warm Peanut-Caramel Dip

¼ cup reduced-fat peanut butter
2 tablespoons fat-free (skim) milk
2 tablespoons fat-free caramel ice cream topping
1 large apple, thinly sliced
4 large pretzel rods, broken in half

1. Combine peanut butter, milk and caramel topping in small saucepan. Heat over low heat, stirring constantly, until mixture is melted and warm.

2. Serve with apple slices and pretzel rods.

Makes 4 servings

Microwave Directions: Combine all ingredients except apple slices and pretzel rods in small microwavable dish. Microwave on MEDIUM (50%) 1 minute; stir well. Microwave an additional minute or until mixture is melted and warm.

Nutrients per Serving (about 1½ tablespoons dip with 4 apple slices and 2 pretzel halves):
Calories: 189, **Calories from Fat:** 29%, **Total Fat:** 6g,
Saturated Fat: 1g, **Cholesterol:** <1mg, **Sodium:** 282mg,
Carbohydrate: 29g, **Dietary Fiber:** 3g, **Protein:** 5g

Dietary Exchanges: 1½ Starch, ½ Fruit, 1 Fat

Warm Peanut-Caramel Dip

wrapped, rolled & skewered

Chicken Wraps

½ **pound boneless skinless chicken thighs**
½ **teaspoon Chinese 5-spice powder**
½ **cup canned bean sprouts, rinsed and drained**
2 **tablespoons sliced almonds**
2 **tablespoons minced green onion**
2 **tablespoons reduced-sodium soy sauce**
4 **teaspoons hoisin sauce**
1 to 2 **teaspoons hot chile sauce with garlic***
4 **large leaves romaine, iceberg or Bibb lettuce**

Hot chile sauce with garlic is available in the Asian foods section of most large supermarkets.

1. Preheat oven to 350°F. Place chicken thighs on baking sheet; sprinkle with 5-spice powder. Bake 20 minutes or until chicken is no longer pink in center. Cool; cut into bite-size pieces.

2. Place chicken, bean sprouts, almonds, green onion, soy sauce, hoisin sauce and chile sauce in large bowl. Stir gently until blended. To serve, spoon ⅓ cup chicken mixture onto each lettuce leaf; roll or fold as desired.

Makes 4 servings

Nutrients per Serving (1 wrap):
Calories: 114, **Calories from Fat:** 24%, **Total Fat:** 5g,
Saturated Fat: 1g, **Cholesterol:** 47mg, **Sodium:** 302mg,
Carbohydrate: 5g, **Dietary Fiber:** 1g, **Protein:** 13g

Dietary Exchanges: 1 Vegetable, 1½ Lean Meat

Greek Spinach-Cheese Rolls

1 package (1 pound) frozen bread dough
1 package (10 ounces) frozen chopped spinach,
    thawed and squeezed dry
¾ cup (3 ounces) crumbled feta cheese
½ cup (2 ounces) shredded reduced-fat Monterey Jack
    cheese
4 green onions, thinly sliced
1 teaspoon dried dill weed
½ teaspoon garlic powder
½ teaspoon black pepper

1. Thaw bread dough according to package directions. Spray 15 standard (2½-inch) muffin cups with nonstick cooking spray; set aside. Roll out dough on lightly floured surface to 15×9-inch rectangle. (If dough is springy and difficult to roll, cover with plastic wrap and let rest 5 minutes to relax.) Position dough so long edge is parallel to edge of work surface.

2. Combine spinach, cheeses, green onions, dill, garlic powder and pepper in large bowl; mix well.

3. Spread spinach mixture evenly over dough to within 1 inch of long edges. Starting at long edge, roll up snugly, pinching seam closed. Cut roll with serrated knife into 15 slices. Place slices, cut sides up, in prepared muffin cups. Cover with plastic wrap; let stand 30 minutes in warm place until rolls are slightly puffy.

4. Preheat oven to 375°F. Bake 20 to 25 minutes or until golden. Serve warm or at room temperature. Rolls can be stored in refrigerator in airtight container up to 2 days.

Makes 15 rolls

Nutrients per Serving (1 roll):
Calories: 111, **Calories from Fat:** 24%, **Total Fat:** 3g,
Saturated Fat: 2g, **Cholesterol:** 8mg, **Sodium:** 267mg,
Carbohydrate: 16g, **Dietary Fiber:** <1g, **Protein:** 5g

Dietary Exchanges: 1 Starch, ½ Lean Meat

Mini Marinated Beef Skewers

  1 boneless beef top sirloin steak (about 1 pound)
  2 tablespoons dry sherry
  2 tablespoons soy sauce
  1 tablespoon dark sesame oil
  2 cloves garlic, minced
18 cherry tomatoes
    Lettuce leaves (optional)

1. Cut beef crosswise into ⅛-inch-thick slices. Place in large resealable food storage bag.

2. Combine sherry, soy sauce, sesame oil and garlic in small bowl; pour over steak in bag. Seal bag; turn to coat. Marinate in refrigerator at least 30 minutes or up to 2 hours. Meanwhile, soak 18 (6-inch) wooden skewers in water 20 minutes.

3. Preheat broiler. Drain beef; discard marinade. Weave beef accordion-style onto skewers. Place on rack of broiler pan. Broil 4 to 5 inches from heat 4 minutes. Turn skewers over; broil 4 minutes or until beef is barely pink in center.

4. Place 1 cherry tomato on end of each skewer; transfer to lettuce-lined platter, if desired. Serve warm or at room temperature. *Makes 9 servings*

Nutrients per Serving (2 skewers):
Calories: 72, **Calories from Fat:** 34%, **Total Fat:** 3g,
Saturated Fat: 1g, **Cholesterol:** 19mg, **Sodium:** 169mg,
Carbohydrate: 2g, **Dietary Fiber:** <1g, **Protein:** 10g

Dietary Exchanges: ½ Vegetable, 1 Lean Meat

Peanut Pitas

8 (6-inch) pita bread rounds, cut in half
16 teaspoons reduced-fat peanut butter
16 teaspoons strawberry fruit spread
1 large banana, thinly sliced (about 48 slices)

1. Spread inside of each pita half with 1 teaspoon peanut butter and 1 teaspoon fruit spread.

2. Fill pita halves evenly with banana slices. Serve immediately. *Makes 8 servings*

Honey Bees: Substitute honey for fruit spread.

Jolly Jellies: Substitute any flavor jelly for fruit spread and thin apple slices for banana slices.

P.B. Crunchers: Substitute reduced-fat mayonnaise for fruit spread and celery slices for banana slices.

Nutrients per Serving (2 Peanut Pita halves):
Calories: 167, **Calories from Fat:** 24%, **Total Fat:** 5g,
Saturated Fat: 1g, **Cholesterol:** 0mg, **Sodium:** 177mg,
Carbohydrate: 26g, **Dietary Fiber:** <1g, **Protein:** 6g

Dietary Exchanges: 2 Starch, ½ Fat

Roast Beef Roll-Ups

2 tablespoons fat-free mayonnaise
½ teaspoon prepared horseradish
2 slices (about 1 ounce each) deli roast beef
6 tablespoons crumbled blue cheese
2 thin slices red onion, quartered

1. Combine mayonnaise and horseradish in small bowl; spread over 1 side of each roast beef slice.

2. Top with blue cheese and onion. Roll up each slice tightly to make 2 rolls. *Makes 2 servings*

Nutrients per Serving (1 roll-up):
Calories: 124, **Calories from Fat:** 51%, **Total Fat:** 7g,
Saturated Fat: 4g, **Cholesterol:** 36mg, **Sodium:** 567mg,
Carbohydrate: 4g, **Dietary Fiber:** 1g, **Protein:** 10g

Dietary Exchanges: ½ Vegetable, 1½ Lean Meat, ½ Fat

Tortellini Teasers

Zesty Tomato Sauce (recipe follows)
½ (9-ounce) package refrigerated cheese tortellini
1 large red or green bell pepper, cut into 1-inch piece
2 medium carrots, cut into ½-inch pieces
1 medium zucchini, cut into ½-inch pieces
12 medium mushrooms
12 cherry tomatoes

1. Prepare Zesty Tomato Sauce; keep warm.

2. Cook tortellini according to package directions; drain.

3. Alternate tortellini and 2 to 3 vegetable pieces on long toothpicks or wooden skewers. Serve as dippers with tomato sauce. *Makes 6 servings*

Zesty Tomato Sauce

1 can (15 ounces) tomato purée
2 tablespoons finely chopped onion
2 tablespoons chopped fresh parsley
1 teaspoon dried oregano
¼ teaspoon dried thyme
¼ teaspoon salt
⅛ teaspoon black pepper

Combine tomato purée, onion, parsley, oregano and thyme in small saucepan. Heat thoroughly, stirring occasionally. Stir in salt and pepper. *Makes 1⅔ cups*

Nutrients per Serving (1 kabob with about ¼ cup Zesty Tomato Sauce):
Calories: 130, **Calories from Fat:** 15%, **Total Fat:** 2g,
Saturated Fat: 1g, **Cholesterol:** 12mg, **Sodium:** 306mg,
Carbohydrate: 23g, **Dietary Fiber:** 5g, **Protein:** 7g

Dietary Exchanges: 1 Starch, 2 Vegetable

Asian Vegetable Rolls with Soy-Lime Dipping Sauce

¼ cup reduced-sodium soy sauce
2 tablespoons lime juice
1 clove garlic, crushed
1 teaspoon honey
½ teaspoon finely chopped fresh ginger
¼ teaspoon dark sesame oil
⅛ to ¼ teaspoon red pepper flakes
½ cup grated cucumber
⅓ cup grated carrot
¼ cup sliced yellow bell pepper (1-inch pieces)
2 tablespoons thinly sliced green onion
18 small lettuce leaves or inner leaves of Bibb
    lettuce head
Sesame seeds (optional)

1. Combine soy sauce, lime juice, garlic, honey, ginger, oil and red pepper flakes in small bowl. Combine cucumber, carrot, bell pepper and green onion in medium bowl. Stir 1 tablespoon soy sauce mixture into vegetable mixture.

2. Place about 1 tablespoon vegetable mixture on each lettuce leaf. Roll up leaves and top with sesame seeds just before serving, if desired. Serve with remaining sauce.

Makes 6 servings

Prep Time: 15 minutes

Nutrients per Serving (3 rolls with 1 tablespoon dipping sauce):
Calories: 25, **Calories from Fat:** 11%, **Total Fat:** <1g,
Saturated Fat: <1g, **Cholesterol:** 0mg, **Sodium:** 343mg,
Carbohydrate: 5g, **Dietary Fiber:** 1g, **Protein:** 1g

Dietary Exchanges: Free

Asian Vegetable Rolls with
Soy-Lime Dipping Sauce

Mexican Roll-Ups

6 uncooked lasagna noodles
¾ cup prepared guacamole
¾ cup chunky salsa
¾ cup (3 ounces) shredded fat-free Cheddar cheese
Additional salsa (optional)

1. Cook lasagna noodles according to package directions, omitting salt. Rinse with cool water; drain.

2. Spread 2 tablespoons guacamole onto each noodle; top with 2 tablespoons salsa and 2 tablespoons cheese.

3. Roll up noodles jelly-roll style. Cut each roll-up in half. Serve immediately with additional salsa, if desired, or cover with plastic wrap and refrigerate up to 3 hours.

Makes 12 servings

Nutrients per Serving (1 roll-up):
Calories: 77, **Calories from Fat:** 28%, **Total Fat:** 1g,
Saturated Fat: 0g, **Cholesterol:** 2mg, **Sodium:** 218mg,
Carbohydrate: 11g, **Dietary Fiber:** 1g, **Protein:** 3g

Dietary Exchanges: 1 Starch

tip

These quick and easy appetizers use prepared guacamole and salsa to save time, but you could easily substitute your own homemade guacamole, salsa and pico de gallo.

Mexican Roll-Ups

stuffed
& topped

Mediterranean Roasted Tomatoes

- 2 small to medium beefsteak tomatoes, cut in half crosswise
- 4 fresh basil leaves
- 2 tablespoons finely chopped pitted kalamata olives
- 2 tablespoons shredded reduced-fat mozzarella cheese
- 2 tablespoons grated Parmesan cheese

1. Preheat toaster oven or oven to broil. Place tomato halves on rack of toaster oven tray or broiler pan. Top each tomato half with 1 fresh basil leaf. Sprinkle olives, mozzarella and Parmesan cheese evenly over all 4 tomato halves.

2. Broil 2 minutes or until cheese melts and begins to brown. Let cool slightly before serving.   *Makes 4 servings*

Nutrients per Serving (1 topped tomato half):
Calories: 34, **Calories from Fat:** 53%, **Total Fat:** 2g, **Saturated Fat:** 1g, **Cholesterol:** 4mg, **Sodium:** 162mg, **Carbohydrate:** 3g, **Dietary Fiber:** 1g, **Protein:** 2g

Dietary Exchanges: ½ Vegetable, ½ Fat

Garden Ratatouille

2 tablespoons extra-virgin olive oil
1 cup chopped sweet onion
1 medium yellow or red bell pepper, diced
4 cloves garlic, minced
1 medium eggplant (about 12 ounces), peeled and
**   diced**
1 can (about 14 ounces) Italian-style stewed tomatoes,
**   undrained, coarsely chopped**
⅓ cup sliced pitted kalamata or black olives
1 tablespoon plus 1½ teaspoons balsamic vinegar
½ teaspoon salt
¼ teaspoon red pepper flakes
¼ cup chopped fresh basil or Italian parsley
8 slices toasted French bread

1. Heat oil in large deep skillet over medium heat. Add onion; cook 5 minutes, stirring occasionally. Add bell pepper and garlic; cook 5 minutes, stirring occasionally. Stir in eggplant, tomatoes with juice and olives. Bring to a boil over high heat. Reduce heat; simmer, covered, 15 minutes or until vegetables are tender.

2. Stir in vinegar, salt and red pepper flakes; cook, uncovered, 2 minutes. Remove from heat; stir in basil. Serve warm or at room temperature on toasted French bread slices.   *Makes 8 servings*

Note: Ratatouille is a classic vegetable stew from the Provençe region of France. Traditionally, it is served as a side dish.

Nutrients per Serving: (1 slice toasted French bread topped with ½ cup ratatouille mixture [¼ cup per slice])
Calories: 180, **Calories from Fat:** 25%, **Total Fat:** 5g,
Saturated Fat: 1g, **Cholesterol:** 0mg, **Sodium:** 583mg,
Carbohydrate: 28g, **Dietary Fiber:** 3g, **Protein:** 5g

Dietary Exchanges: 1 Starch, 2½ Vegetable, 1 Fat

Tortilla "Pizza"

1 can (about 14 ounces) Mexican-style stewed
tomatoes, drained
1 can (10 ounces) chunk white chicken packed in
water, drained
1 green onion, minced
2 teaspoons ground cumin, divided
½ teaspoon garlic powder
1 cup fat-free refried beans
4 tablespoons chopped fresh cilantro, divided
2 large or 4 small flour tortillas
1 cup (4 ounces) shredded Monterey Jack cheese with
jalapeño peppers

1. Preheat broiler.

2. Combine tomatoes, chicken, green onion, 1 teaspoon
cumin and garlic powder in medium bowl; mix well.
Combine refried beans, remaining 1 teaspoon cumin and
2 tablespoons cilantro in small bowl. Set aside.

3. Place tortillas on baking sheet. Broil 30 seconds per side
or until crisp but not browned. Remove from oven. *Reduce
oven temperature to 400°F.*

4. Spread bean mixture evenly over each tortilla. Top with
chicken mixture and cheese. Bake 5 minutes.

5. *Return oven to broil.* Broil tortillas 2 to 3 minutes or until
cheese melts. Top with remaining 2 tablespoons cilantro.
Serve immediately. *Makes 8 servings*

Nutrients per Serving (1 wedge [¼ of 1 large Tortilla "Pizza" or
½ of 1 small Tortilla "Pizza"]):
Calories: 185, **Calories from Fat:** 34%, **Total Fat:** 7g,
Saturated Fat: 3g, **Cholesterol:** 31mg, **Sodium:** 604mg,
Carbohydrate: 19g, **Dietary Fiber:** 3g, **Protein:** 13g

Dietary Exchanges: 1 Starch, 1 Vegetable, 1½ Lean Meat

Blue Crab Stuffed Tomatoes

½ **pound Florida blue crabmeat**
10 **plum tomatoes**
½ **cup finely chopped celery**
⅓ **cup plain low-fat yogurt**
2 **tablespoons minced green onion**
2 **tablespoons finely chopped red bell pepper**
½ **teaspoon lemon juice**
¼ **teaspoon salt**
⅛ **teaspoon black pepper**

Remove any shell or cartilage from crabmeat.

Cut tomatoes in half lengthwise. Carefully scoop out centers of tomatoes; discard pulp. Invert on paper towels.

Combine crabmeat, celery, yogurt, onion, red bell pepper, lemon juice, salt and black pepper. Mix well.

Fill tomato halves with crab mixture. Refrigerate 2 hours.

Makes 20 appetizers

*Favorite recipe from **Florida Department of Agriculture and Consumer Services, Bureau of Seafood and Aquaculture***

Nutrients per Serving (1 stuffed tomato):
Calories: 46, **Calories from Fat:** 12%, **Total Fat:** 1g,
Saturated Fat: <1g, **Cholesterol:** 27mg, **Sodium:** 138mg,
Carbohydrate: 3g, **Dietary Fiber:** 1g, **Protein:** 7g

Dietary Exchanges: ½ Vegetable, 1 Lean Meat

Blue Crab Stuffed Tomatoes

Cheesy Potato Skin Appetizers

⅔ cup Zesty Pico de Gallo (page 50) or purchased
　　salsa
5 potatoes (4 to 5 ounces each)
　　Butter-flavored cooking spray
½ (8-ounce) package reduced-fat cream cheese
2 tablespoons reduced-fat sour cream
⅓ cup shredded reduced-fat sharp Cheddar cheese
2 tablespoons sliced black olives (optional)
¼ cup minced fresh cilantro (optional)

1. Prepare Zesty Pico de Gallo; cover and refrigerate.

2. Preheat oven to 425°F. Scrub potatoes; pierce several times with fork. Bake 45 minutes or until soft. Cool.

3. Cut each potato in half lengthwise. Scoop out insides of potatoes with spoon, leaving ¼-inch-thick shell. (Reserve insides for another use, if desired.) Place potato skins on baking sheet; spray lightly with cooking spray.

4. Preheat broiler. Broil potato skins 6 inches from heat 5 minutes or until lightly browned and crisp.

5. *Reduce oven temperature to 350°F.* Combine cream cheese and sour cream in small bowl; stir until well blended. Divide evenly among potato skins; spread to cover. Top with Zesty Pico de Gallo, cheese and olives, if desired. Bake 15 minutes or until heated through. Sprinkle with cilantro.

Makes 10 servings

continued on page 50

Cheesy Potato Skin Appetizers, continued

Zesty Pico de Gallo

> 2 cups chopped seeded tomatoes
> 1 cup chopped green onions
> 1 can (8 ounces) tomato sauce
> ½ cup minced fresh cilantro
> 1 to 2 tablespoons minced jalapeño peppers*
> 1 tablespoon fresh lime juice

Jalapeño peppers can sting and irritate the skin, so wear rubber gloves when handling peppers and do not touch your eyes.

Combine all ingredients in medium bowl. Cover; refrigerate at least 1 hour.   *Makes 4 cups*

Nutrients per Serving (1 potato skin appetizer with about 1 tablespoon pico de gallo):
Calories: 86, **Calories from Fat:** 10%, **Total Fat:** 1g, **Saturated Fat:** 1g, **Cholesterol:** 4mg, **Sodium:** 149mg, **Carbohydrate:** 15g, **Dietary Fiber:** 3g, **Protein:** 4g

Dietary Exchanges: 1 Starch

Instant Individual Pizza

> 1 (6-inch) whole wheat tortilla
> 1 tablespoon no-salt-added tomato sauce
> ¼ teaspoon dried oregano
> 2 tablespoons shredded reduced-fat Swiss cheese

Preheat oven to 500°F. Place tortilla on baking sheet. Spread tomato sauce over tortilla to edge. Sprinkle with oregano. Top with cheese. Bake 5 minutes or until tortilla is crisp and cheese is bubbly.   *Makes 1 serving*

Nutrients per Serving (1 pizza):
Calories: 106, **Calories from Fat:** 19%, **Total Fat:** 2g, **Saturated Fat:** 1g, **Cholesterol:** 8mg, **Sodium:** 208mg, **Carbohydrate:** 13g, **Dietary Fiber:** 9g, **Protein:** 7g

Dietary Exchanges: 1 Starch, ½ Lean Meat

Super Nachos

12 large baked low-fat tortilla chips (about 1½ ounces)
½ cup (2 ounces) shredded reduced-fat Cheddar cheese
¼ cup fat-free refried beans
2 tablespoons chunky salsa

MICROWAVE DIRECTIONS

1. Arrange chips in single layer on large microwavable plate. Sprinkle cheese evenly over chips.

2. Spoon 1 teaspoon beans over each chip; top with ½ teaspoon salsa.

3. Microwave on MEDIUM (50%) 1½ minutes; rotate dish. Microwave 1 to 1½ minutes more or until cheese is melted.

Makes 2 servings

Conventional Directions: Preheat oven to 350°F. Substitute foil-covered baking sheet for microwavable plate. Assemble nachos on prepared baking sheet as directed above. Bake 10 to 12 minutes or until cheese is melted.

Nutrients per Serving (6 nachos):
Calories: 165, **Calories from Fat:** 44%, **Total Fat:** 8g, **Saturated Fat:** 5g, **Cholesterol:** 20mg, **Sodium:** 526mg, **Carbohydrate:** 13g, **Dietary Fiber:** 2g, **Protein:** 9g

Dietary Exchanges: 1 Starch, 1 Lean Meat, 1 Fat

BLT Cukes

3 slices crisp-cooked bacon, crumbled
½ cup finely chopped lettuce
½ cup finely chopped baby spinach
¼ cup diced tomato
1 tablespoon plus 1½ teaspoons fat-free mayonnaise
⅛ teaspoon salt (optional)
¼ teaspoon black pepper (optional)
1 large cucumber
  Snipped green onion or minced fresh parsley
    (optional)

1. Combine bacon, lettuce, spinach, tomato and mayonnaise in medium bowl. Season with salt and pepper, if desired; set aside.

2. Peel cucumber. Trim off ends and cut in half lengthwise. Use spoon to scoop out seeds; discard seeds. Divide bacon mixture between cucumber halves, mounding in hollowed areas. Garnish with parsley. Cut into 2-inch pieces.

Makes 8 to 10 pieces

Note: Make these snacks when cucumbers are plentiful and large enough to easily hollow out with a spoon. You can make these up to 12 hours ahead of time.

Nutrients per Serving (1 piece):
Calories: 26, **Calories from Fat:** 50%, **Total Fat:** 2g,
Saturated Fat: <1g, **Cholesterol:** 3mg, **Sodium:** 72mg,
Carbohydrate: 2g, **Dietary Fiber:** <1g, **Protein:** 2g

Dietary Exchanges: Free

by the handful

Rosemary-Scented Nut Mix

2 tablespoons unsalted butter
2 cups pecan halves
1 cup unsalted macadamia nuts
1 cup walnuts
1 teaspoon dried rosemary, crushed
½ teaspoon salt
¼ teaspoon red pepper flakes

1. Preheat oven to 300°F. Melt butter in large saucepan over low heat. Add pecans, macadamia nuts and walnuts; mix well. Add rosemary, salt and red pepper flakes; cook and stir about 1 minute.

2. Spread mixture onto ungreased nonstick baking sheet. Bake 15 minutes, stirring mixture occasionally. Cool completely on baking sheet on wire rack.

Makes 32 servings

Nutrients per Serving (2 tablespoons mix):
Calories: 108, **Calories from Fat:** 88%, **Total Fat:** 11g,
Saturated Fat: 2g, **Cholesterol:** 2mg, **Sodium:** 37mg,
Carbohydrate: 2g, **Dietary Fiber:** 1g, **Protein:** 2g

Dietary Exchanges: 2 Fat

Peppy Snack Mix

3 (3-inch) plain rice cakes, broken into bite-size pieces
1½ cups bite-size frosted shredded wheat biscuit cereal
¾ cup pretzel sticks, halved
3 tablespoons reduced-fat margarine, melted
2 teaspoons reduced-sodium Worcestershire sauce
¾ teaspoon chili powder
⅛ to ¼ teaspoon ground red pepper

1. Preheat oven to 300°F.

2. Combine rice cake pieces, cereal and pretzels in 13×9-inch baking pan.

3. Combine margarine, Worcestershire, chili powder and red pepper in small bowl. Drizzle over cereal mixture in pan; toss to combine. Bake 20 minutes, stirring once.

Makes 6 servings

Nutrients per Serving (⅔ cup snack mix):
Calories: 118, **Calories from Fat:** 25%, **Total Fat:** 3g,
Saturated Fat: 1g, **Cholesterol:** 0mg, **Sodium:** 156mg,
Carbohydrate: 20g, **Dietary Fiber:** 1g, **Protein:** 2g

Dietary Exchanges: 1½ Starch, ½ Fat

Worcestershire sauce is a dark, savory sauce developed in India and named after the English town, Worcester, where it was first bottled. It has a very unique, complex flavor that is difficult to substitute.

Cinnamon Caramel Corn

8 cups air-popped popcorn (about ⅓ cup kernels)
2 tablespoons honey
4 teaspoons butter
¼ teaspoon ground cinnamon

1. Preheat oven to 350°F. Spray jelly-roll pan with nonstick cooking spray. Place popcorn in large bowl.

2. Cook and stir honey, butter and cinnamon in small saucepan over low heat until butter is melted and mixture is smooth; immediately pour over popcorn. Toss to coat evenly. Pour onto prepared pan; bake 12 to 14 minutes or until coating is golden brown and appears crackled, stirring twice during baking time.

3. Let cool on pan 5 minutes. (As popcorn cools, coating becomes crisp. If not crisp enough, or if popcorn softens upon standing, return to oven and heat 5 to 8 minutes.)

Makes 4 servings

Cajun Popcorn: Preheat oven and prepare jelly-roll pan as directed above. Combine 7 teaspoons honey, 4 teaspoons butter and 1 teaspoon Cajun or Creole seasoning in small saucepan. Proceed with recipe as directed above. Makes 4 servings.

Italian Popcorn: Spray 8 cups of air-popped popcorn with fat-free butter-flavored spray to coat. Sprinkle with 2 tablespoons finely grated Parmesan cheese, ⅛ teaspoon black pepper and ½ teaspoon dried oregano; toss to coat. Makes 4 servings.

Nutrients per Serving (2 cups Cinnamon Caramel Corn):
Calories: 117, **Calories from Fat:** 29%, **Total Fat:** 4g,
Saturated Fat: 1g, **Cholesterol:** 0mg, **Sodium:** 45mg,
Carbohydrate: 19g, **Dietary Fiber:** 1g, **Protein:** 2g

Dietary Exchanges: 1 Starch, 1 Fat

Clockwise from top: Italian Popcorn, Cinnamon Caramel Corn and Cajun Popcorn

Bite-You-Back Roasted Edamame

2 teaspoons vegetable oil
2 teaspoons honey
¼ teaspoon wasabi powder*
1 package (10 ounces) ready-to-eat shelled edamame
   Kosher salt (optional)

Available in the Asian section of most supermarkets and in Asian specialty markets.

1. Preheat oven to 375°F.

2. Stir together oil, honey and wasabi powder in large bowl. Add edamame; toss to coat. Transfer to baking sheet; arrange in single layer.

3. Bake 12 to 15 minutes or until edamame are golden brown, stirring once. Remove from baking sheet immediately; sprinkle with salt, if desired. Cool completely.

4. After popcorn has cooled completely, store in airtight container until ready to serve.   *Makes 4 servings*

Nutrients per Serving (½ cup [without added salt]):
Calories: 78, **Calories from Fat:** 29%, **Total Fat:** 4g,
Saturated Fat: 1g, **Cholesterol:** 0mg, **Sodium:** 7mg,
Carbohydrate: 7g, **Dietary Fiber:** 1g, **Protein:** 4g

Dietary Exchanges: 1½ Vegetable, ½ Fat

Bite-You-Back Roasted Edamame

Southwest Snack Mix

4 cups corn cereal squares
2 cups unsalted pretzels
½ cup unsalted pumpkin or squash seeds
1½ teaspoons chili powder
1 teaspoon minced fresh cilantro or parsley
½ teaspoon garlic powder
½ teaspoon onion powder
1 egg white
2 tablespoons olive oil
2 tablespoons lime juice

1. Preheat oven to 300°F. Spray large nonstick baking sheet with nonstick cooking spray; set aside.

2. Combine cereal, pretzels and pumpkin seeds in large bowl. Combine chili powder, cilantro, garlic powder and onion powder in small bowl.

3. Whisk together egg white, oil and lime juice in separate small bowl. Pour over cereal mixture in large bowl; toss to coat evenly. Add seasoning mixture; mix lightly to coat evenly. Transfer to prepared baking sheet.

4. Bake 45 minutes, stirring every 15 minutes; cool. Store in airtight container.   *Makes about 12 servings*

Variation: Substitute ½ cup unsalted peanuts for pumpkin seeds.

Nutrients per Serving (½ cup snack mix):
Calories: 93, **Calories from Fat:** 28%, **Total Fat:** 3g, **Saturated Fat:** <1g, **Cholesterol:** 0mg, **Sodium:** 114mg, **Carbohydrate:** 15g, **Dietary Fiber:** 1g, **Protein:** 2g

Dietary Exchanges: 1 Starch, ½ Fat

acknowledgments

The publisher would like to thank the companies and organizations listed below for the use of their recipes and photographs in this publication.

Dole Food Company, Inc.

Florida Department of Agriculture and Consumer Services, Bureau of Seafood and Aquaculture